From Seed To Apple

Inspirational stories from Washington's classrooms, featuring the Teachers, Principals, and Classified School Employees of the Year

VOLUME XII

2022

Disclaimer and Copyright Statement and Policy

This volume of From Seed to Apple is dedicated to the educators, families, and students of Washington— especially the class of 2022. You have shown us what grit looks like and have fought for the right to a quality education. Despite enormous challenges, you have demonstrated a passion for education, the will to persevere, and a determination to grow and even thrive.

This collection is just a glimpse into our schools. It may be a new perspective for some and familiar territory for others. We hope, whoever you are, you will find encouragement in these stories and optimism for our future.

Table of Contents

BROOKE BROWN

2021 Washington State Teacher of the Year

Washington High School
Franklin Pierce School District

Foreword

2021...the year that needs no introduction

I have learned a great deal as Washington's State Teacher of the Year, during this unprecedented year. I have seen educators across the state, who are some of the hardest working people I know, somehow manage to work even harder. To show up every day and love our students in the midst of their own struggles. I have seen our students and educators excel and struggle, grieve and experience joy amidst a pandemic where so much feels uncertain.

We have come a long way, and we have long way to go. We can't continue to do more of what wasn't working pre-pandemic. We have to collectively weave a new way of doing school, together. We have to leverage the brilliance of our families and community members to serve our students in a new way. Utilizing the creativity of all involved to build deeper partnerships with educators and family members to create opportunities for young people to show up as their full selves, removing barriers and supporting them in what they need to thrive.

Inspirational stories from Washington's classrooms, featuring the Teachers, Principals, and Classified School Employees of the Year

ix

In education, we have the opportunity to disrupt predictable outcomes for students who have been historically left out. Stories are an important way to learn about one another and bear witness to one another's experiences. Humbling ourselves, leaning in and being willing to learn from others is how we begin to build community. We understand that no one is disposable. Everyone has dignity and worth, and we must work together to build that future that fits all of us—all of humanity and nature. We can do it, but we have to do it together.

The stories in this 12th edition are just a few snapshots of the beautiful community that are built in the classrooms across our state. The work of education is a love letter to our students. We see you, we value you, and we will do what needs to be done to help you live your best life. You deserve it all!

THIEN NGUYEN

Student

Mariner High School
Mukilteo School District

The Power of Language
An immigrant's learning experience

"CON ĐI QUA MỸ [I'm going to America]," I shout to my extended family with tears dropping down onto the reflective floors of Đà Nẵng Airport. With every step forward, my cousins, aunts, and maternal grandma Lieu take a step in the other direction until I am on my 16-hour long flight, and they are back in the little run-down building I used to love calling home. That marks the beginning of a new adventure in my life—one that will be in the "Promised Land."

It has been more than 13 years since I left Vietnam, 13 long years of me experiencing the sheer horrors—and joys—of what it has been like living here. Back then, four-year-old me had left with a preschool understanding of the Vietnamese language. "Thưa cô! Thưa chú! [Hi, ma'am! Hi, sir!]" I remember excitedly saying to the adults I met out on the streets near my home. I picked up Vietnamese well at an early stage of my life, mimicking the words I heard my parents use to converse with others; although, I sometimes would never know what some of the words meant. And after enrolling in an elementary school in Washington

Inspirational stories from Washington's classrooms, featuring the Teachers, Principals, and Classified School Employees of the Year

1

state, I would add English into my mixing pot of languages. As I gradually mixed and mixed, I would lose my ability to converse proficiently in my mother tongue.

This hurt so much.

I lost a part of my identity—the only thing that kept me rooted in the home I left behind. That not only devastated me but my parents too, who have difficulty understanding my broken Vietnamese. They still, to this day, continue to struggle with comprehending the Vietnamese words that come out of my mouth.

"Con đang nói gì vậy [What are you saying]?"

The door slams. A noise that loudly echoes throughout the entire two-story house when I cannot get my parents to understand me. It happens so often that my parents and I share limited basic conversations now; they ask if I am hungry, tired, or what I am doing to which I respond in utter frustration, "con được rồi, đi ra phòng đi! [I'm okay, please leave]."

I do not want to be mad at them all the time, so I run away as fast as I possibly can.

And by the time my legs give up on me, I end up in the arms of my closest friends. With their comforting voices and soft touch, I feel as though they are my real family—one that I can speak to with no language barrier whatsoever. I hope to continue to include new members into my ever-growing "family." My daily "hello!" puts a smile on my friends' faces, and I am no longer reminded of my struggle to converse with my parents; no longer reminded of the pain I feel in my guilty heart after simultaneously switching between Vietnamese and English because I just could not find the right words to use.

I will never forget my Vietnamese, but as I continue to befriend more English-speakers, I feel emboldened to show the world what my English skills have truly done for me. That is why I want to become a language teacher one day. With first-hand knowledge of the difficulty of learning a new language in a foreign country, I can reassure my future students that it is perfectly natural to struggle with losing their native tongue. It happened to me, and it can happen to anyone.

And while I am on my journey of teaching, I hope to relearn Vietnamese, so conversations with my parents no longer end in the slamming of a door. It will end with a deeper connection formed between my parents and me.

Despite all the challenges you might face in life, your home is wherever and whatever you make of it. The people who have constantly challenged me to be the best that I can be are the people I wish to continue surrounding myself with—my parents included.

"Xin lỗi ba mẹ. Con không muốn la nữa. [Sorry mom and dad. I don't want to yell anymore]."

Inspirational stories from Washington's classrooms, featuring the Teachers, Principals, and Classified School Employees of the Year

3

NANCY BALDWIN

2021 Washington State Classified School Employee of the Year

Kelso School District

We All Want the Same Things
A story of triumph over adversity

No child grows up thinking, I want to be homeless when I grow up. They have dreams of becoming a teacher, a counselor, a welder, or even the president, or like my student Katie they want to become a police officer. As children, we all want the same things: a safe place to live, clean clothes, enough food to eat every day, an adult in their life to guide them, to have a person celebrate their birthday, someone to tell them they matter, to drive a car, to go to prom, to feel accepted and valued. All kids need someone in their life to share their accomplishments, happiness, and sadness with. But sadly, that is not always the hand life deals us. This world has so many barriers, but even more for those who do not have the skills or the means to make ends meet.

Every morning, I post the thought or quote for the week on the whiteboard. The beginning of this story starts with a quote from Brene Brown, "Vulnerability is not winning or losing; it's having the courage to show up and be seen when we have no control over the outcome. Vulnerability is not weakness; it's our

Inspirational stories from Washington's classrooms, featuring the Teachers, Principals, and Classified School Employees of the Year

5

greatest measure of courage." It is a bit ominous knowing now what came the next day.

The week before COVID-19 forced our schools to close in 2020, I was watching and listening to the news reports and saw the writing on the walls. I sat in my classroom, and asked myself, "How I am going to assist in keeping my students and families safe?" They already face uphill battles daily. Many are struggling with poor health, homelessness, and food insecurities without any additional challenges. My students and their families were already living in a pandemic state of mind with no job, not enough food in the cupboards, eviction, or worse. In many ways my families taught me how to adapt to the new reality we were facing. What I have learned is that we were now stepping into the world they were remarkably familiar with, a world of desperation.

The morning bell had just rung, my door opened wide, and Katie ran in with a look of panic on her face. I said, "Honey, what's wrong?" She came closer to me and said, "I keep hearing about this new virus." I told her, "It's going to be all right. We are going to get things in place just in case we are out of school for a few days." She stopped me and said, "I'm not worried about me, I know how to survive, I am worried about you!"

This child, on this day, took my breath away. In the face of her own uncertain future, with so much trauma in her own path, she was worried about me. This was the moment I knew this job was so much bigger than the plans I had for myself.

What I have learned since March 2020 is that the McKinney-Vento and unaccompanied minor students and their families were able to adapt to the pandemic challenges with calmness.

These crises were foreign to those of us accustomed to stable housing, reliable employment, and a dependable social safety net but all too familiar to them. They were able to make the necessary changes to their daily routine with ease and keep moving forward. They were able to persevere and even help others adjust to the new COVID normal of our time.

After spending months in quarantine and having been deprived of the things that made us who we are, my girl Katie, with all she had faced was happier than ever to return to school when restrictions were lifted. Kelso High School was a routine for Katie. School is a safe space and allows Katie to feel normal and accepted. She was so excited to be back and walked through the doors as though she never missed a step. Katie worked hard, sometimes stumbling but always able to catch herself before hitting the ground.

When graduation came, I watched her carry herself across the stage on that beautiful day with purpose even though no family was present to celebrate her success. Katie was proud, courageous, confident, fearless, and determined to keep moving. The world was hers at that moment in time. Nothing was going to get in her way. She had found her voice, her direction, her reason to be. This was her school, these were her classmates, and she finally felt like she deserved to belong.

After the ceremony, she ran into my arms and hugged me so tightly, both of us crying, neither one of us wanting to let the other go, both knowing this may be the last time we would share a moment. Katie whispered in my ear that she had come to me broken, and I put her back together.

Inspirational stories from Washington's classrooms, featuring the Teachers, Principals, and Classified School Employees of the Year

7

The truth is it was the system that was put in place to protect her that was broken.

Not so long ago this child came to me as an unaccompanied minor, unsure, anxious, eating her lunch in the bathroom and silent. Katie and I met in a moment of crisis, but by the time she was ready to leave she was determined to no longer be a victim. She fell seven times but stood up eight, she found her footing, her passion, and she did it her way. She was able to help me overcome obstacles that she had mastered: an uncertain tomorrow, loss of income, food shortages, isolation, and the fear of not being able to control my own future. This child is brilliant, it's now time for her to show the world.

Graduation is just the beginning of Katie's story, and I am so honored to have been invited along. She has been accepted into community college and is one step closer to achieving her dream of becoming a police officer. When she completes her training and prepares for the academy graduation, you can bet I will be there to share in her accomplishment. I hope when she thinks back on the journey we shared, she smiles and feels a sense of pride in how far she has come.

Katie taught me to let my students set the pace. When they stumble, we stop, we wait, and when we are stable again, we continue our journey forward. I now meet each student where they are. I have learned to listen with my heart, to celebrate our similarities and embrace our differences, to see things through their eyes, and to always give grace. Katie has incredible assets that can benefit her fellow students especially at this moment when those with comfortable lives are experiencing discomfort for the first time. Katie is a student that has set a true example for others to follow in our community. We can all learn from her experiences even without having lived with such adversity ourselves. By inviting those with different experiences into our lives, we see their gifts. Katie has had to develop her own special set of skills to survive in this world. I constantly find myself talking to students and encouraging them to realize their value, find the courage to get into the arena, and use their gifts to create their narrative and tell their own stories.

Inspirational stories from Washington's classrooms, featuring the Teachers, Principals, and Classified School Employees of the Year

9

BOO BALKAN FOSTER
(APACHE/ADOPTED MAKAH)

2022 Puget Sound ESD Regional Teacher of the Year

Native Education - Title VI Program partnering with Chief Sealth International High School & Denny International Middle School Seattle Public Schools

Still Here

The continued fight for Native visibility

"How was your day?" I asked my 8- and 9-year-old daughters as we drove home from after school care. My 9-year-old was upset as she shared sadly, "My baby died." Trying to guard my surprise as to what a baby dying had to do with anything related to school, the conversation continued. Not only did I learn how—yes—her baby in her role as a pioneer woman had died, but I also watched in my rearview mirror as she grabbed my 8-year old's head and taught her what scalping was. It is a day I relive in my head. I am tired. So tired. However, it is this moment and many others that push me forward as an educator. I fight because I can. Following is the letter I sent her teacher:

> *Dear Ms. _____,*
>
> *I am writing this letter from my personal email because I want to make it clear I am writing as a parent and not a Seattle School District teacher.*

Inspirational stories from Washington's classrooms, featuring the Teachers, Principals, and Classified School Employees of the Year

11

Frankly, even as a seasoned educator of over two decades, I am not confidant I even have the words to convey my angst, concern, and frustration.

Tonight, as I drove my daughters home, Rxxxx shared that today in her role as a "pioneer," her baby died. I gasped. How horrific. She then continued and told me some people called "hot-heads" (she'd never heard the term before) had snuck off and killed some Indians. In fact, they had scalped them. I listened in horror as she explained to her 8-year-old sister what scalping was. I was dumbfounded. She then told me her group was to decide how they would respond to the scalpers. She told me they first decided to shoot them in their limbs so they could not do it again. Then, they decided to burn them alive.

Thankfully, I was already in our driveway or else I would've had to pull to the side of the road. Her words hit me in the gut, and I struggled to respond. I simply said, "I hate this." Sensing my angst, Rxxxx assured me they were learning the pioneers were bad. She assured me they were learning some of the same things she had learned at home, and then she burst into tears.

Please know my frustration is not with you personally as a teacher. As a parent (and educator) I appreciate the care you give my girls. I simply think there has to be a better way. Earlier in the year, I brought up my concerns and stated for comparisons sake, we don't ask Black students to take the role of "Masters", nor do we ask Jewish students to take the role of Nazis. As I stated previously, I don't have the words and I am admittedly struggling but there is something that doesn't feel right here.

I appreciate looking at things from a variety of perspectives. I get it. We need critical thinkers with compassionate hearts more than ever. Also, it is not lost on me as a mixed blooded woman that my ancestors stole my ancestors land, my ancestors raped my ancestors and yes, very likely there was some scalping too; however, I'm not convinced exposing my 9-year-old in this manner is appropriate or increases her understanding of "Western Expansion." Personally, I've always looked at this time facing east.*

Admittedly, I am not involved with my children's curriculum as much as I wish I were. I spend all day caring for other peoples' children and am filled with guilt as I worry I neglect my own. Today added in anxiety. And anger. My 9-year-old is developmentally still a concrete thinker. I appreciate the nuances and gray areas in history. I am not sure she can.

Finally, as my husband reminds me, this issue is much bigger than Rxxxx's class. As our precious 4th graders play "pioneer," as the protagonists they are inherently the good guys. I believe this exercise creates "the other" and contributes to what I deal with every day as a Native woman,

Inspirational stories from Washington's classrooms, featuring the Teachers, Principals, and Classified School Employees of the Year

13

mother, and educator. We are not so much "the
other." We are the invisible.

Thank you for listening to my concerns.

Respectfully,

Boo Balkan Foster
Mama to Rxxxx and Bxxxx Foster
Apache/Adopted Makah

This letter was sent four years ago to my child's teacher, and I never received a response. Eventually, at my insistence, I met with the principal with the support of the Native Education Department Manager. She was told they didn't respond due to "white fright." I was also told the curriculum was approved. This did not ease my angst or alleviate my concerns. Quite the contrary. Harm to my child was never addressed. Harm to the non-native children in the classroom was never addressed. I was not satisfied.

I worked with my support systems and eventually with the support of the Director of Curriculum, the curriculum was pulled from the approved list; however, this was not done without protest. Educators protested because, "kids like it." I honestly didn't have words to respond. I do now but I fear they fall on deaf ears. Or perhaps hard, unfeeling hearts. Imagine how differently this scenario would've played out if, instead of simulating scalping, my daughter simulated lynching. Both horrific; yet, somehow, one is more acceptable because it ties in with white settler supremacy stories of our nation's founding.

These issues are brought to educators' attention regularly, but because Native peoples are so relegated to the past in most of our curriculum and otherwise, educators don't know how to respond. Often, as in the case mentioned, they simply don't. Harm goes unaddressed and Natives continue to be relegated to the past. With the inaction, educators are complicit in making Native people invisible. Yet, we are still here!

It can be challenging to know how to respond when such instances arise. Fortunately, Washington state has mandated the teaching of the Since Time Immemorial curriculum through Senate Bill 5433. We can begin by teaching it. The curriculum is endorsed by all 29 federally recognized tribes in Washington state; and yet, currently, there is no framework to ensure it is utilized by educators. The curriculum steps away from stereotypes and moves into contemporary contributions of Native nations. If we teach Since Time Immemorial in our schools one less parent may have to watch as their 9-year-old demonstrates to a younger sibling what scalping is from the rearview mirror after asking about their child's day.

Instead, we can celebrate the richness that continues to be Washington state. We ensure our children are not only taught the truth, but also the ways our citizens have worked in partnership with the land, and in partnership with each other to create the amazing place we all call home.

* "Facing east" is a reference to those who were already here and looking eastward as newcomers came to these lands. Imagine what that looked like? Westward expansion often ignores Native peoples were (and continue to be) here. Thank you to JR for asking me to explain this term. It was obvious to me, and I appreciate the ask.

Inspirational stories from Washington's classrooms, featuring the Teachers, Principals, and Classified School Employees of the Year

15

LINDA JOHNSON

2022 ESD 123 Regional Teacher of the Year

Early Learning Center
Richland School District

A Change of Heart

How glimmers of hope and celebrations of joy helped a teacher discover her passion

I entered my principal's office, shut the door firmly, and collapsed into the chair next to his desk. He turned from his computer with surprise in his eyes. I had never done this before and clearly had his full attention. "How can I help?" he asked. With tears threatening to spill from my eyes and run down my face, I wondered how I would even begin to answer that question. My stomach was in knots as I realized my world was ending, yet beginning, both at the same time. Articulating my emotions seemed next to impossible, there was so much I needed to say. "I'm leaving," I stated simply. Two words. Then the dam burst, and I dissolved into tears.

I began teaching with my district in 1992 and had been teaching for 23 years when my professional life took an unexpected turn. You see, I had been a kindergarten teacher for the majority of my career. It was my life-long goal. It was my identity. Not just any kindergarten teacher, but a Sacajawea Elementary kindergarten teacher. I proudly taught in the elementary

Inspirational stories from Washington's classrooms, featuring the Teachers, Principals, and Classified School Employees of the Year

17

school that I attended as a kindergarten through 6th grade student and where I did my student teaching—in kindergarten, of course. I knew my grade level, became a leader among my peers, and was certain that I was destined to teach and retire as a kindergarten teacher at Sacajawea. I was fully immersed in the school community, had built trusting relationships with the families and staff, and was a leader on the district planning team for the much-anticipated move from half-day to full-day kindergarten. The plans were glorious, and I couldn't wait to jump-in with everything I had to join my team on this new and exciting adventure.

This adventure was not to be for me, however, and I was devastated. The unforeseen twist? I had chosen to teach half-time for the past five years in order to enjoy the best of both worlds—teaching and raising my children. That put me at the bottom of the applicant pool for a full-time kindergarten position, regardless of my seniority and current position in the building. Another teacher had transferred into "my job" before I could even be considered.

This event shook my world, rattled my identity, and sent me into a state of confusion and anxiety. To make matters worse, I was asked to decide—quickly—which of the remaining positions I wanted to accept. My current position would no longer exist once the year was over. Half-time kindergarten classrooms had come to an end. I felt torn as I weighed the pros and cons of both positions. I could take an open full-time kindergarten position at a different school, but that lacked the history and relationships that kept me at Sacajawea. Or I could take the half-time preschool position at Sacajawea, but that lacked the love I had for teaching kindergarten. After many sleepless nights, and way too many internal conversations with myself, I decided that I just couldn't leave my Sacajawea community. Preschool it was. It would be fine; it had to be.

I was nervous about the change. I'd never taught 3- and 4-year-old children. I was sure I would miss the academic content and student growth that attracted me to kindergarten. Adding insult to injury, several weeks later the position suddenly moved from one session to two sessions. I'd ironically been asked to apply for, and move into, a full-time contract because no one else was interested in the afternoon position. I couldn't help but wonder why and questioned what I had gotten myself into.

The answer to, "What had I gotten myself into?" was the absolute hardest teaching position that I've ever had in my entire life. The reason the position had become full-time was because our district had been awarded additional Early Childhood Education Assistance Program (ECEAP) student spots through an expansion grant from the Department of Early Learning (DEL—now renamed the Department of Children, Youth, and Families). This program would be run through our district in partnership with the Office of Superintendent of Public Instruction and DEL. It brought with it an astonishing number of trainings, certifications, evaluations, data collection tools, and program expectations.

I told myself to give it a year—I could do anything for a year—and dove in headfirst. Little did I know how tough that year would be. That learning the overwhelming regulations associated with running the program would bring me to tears a minimum of three times a week. That the expectations of a multitude of teacher and classroom evaluations for both agencies would cause me to lose sleep night after night. That the mountain

Inspirational stories from Washington's classrooms, featuring the Teachers, Principals, and Classified School Employees of the Year

19

of paperwork expected for student assessment and program standards would take over my evenings and weekends.

As I became more confident in my abilities, however, things slowly began to change. The expectations didn't go away, but I learned how to complete the procedural and data collection aspects of the position more efficiently. I sought out colleagues, and we figured out how to share the load. I became a leader within my group and mentored those who were new to the position—striving to make their transition easier than mine. I discovered how to learn, be curious, investigate, and grow through the eyes of my young students. The academic content and student growth I'd feared I would miss? It was embedded in each and every thing we experienced together. Oh, how smart and insightful my students were! There were glimmers of hope that turned into joy. So much joy.

The most beautiful aspect of an ECEAP program is that, as a teacher, you develop a deep connection with both your students and their families. You create a strong community together. The philosophy of the program is early intervention for families as well as their young children. We connect families with resources to meet their basic needs. We ensure that our families are physically and emotionally safe. We work together as a team on student and family goals. We strive to help families break the cycle of poverty and move towards self-sufficiency. We join them on this journey and support them as they grow. We become each other's family.

There are so many glimmers of hope that transform into enormous celebrations of joy. A child who enters our classroom as a shy 3-year-old clinging to his parent's leg and leaves as a self-assured 5-year-old ready to take on kindergarten. A student who initially has no idea how to hold a pencil and learns to draw and write by the year's end. A child who joins our classroom needing strategies for self-regulation and leaves able to express her emotions and work with perseverance.

The celebrations aren't limited to the growth we see in the children. We also cheer for the parent who receives a grant to go back to school and returns to tell us that he has graduated and has a job offer in his preferred field. For the family who received financial counseling, followed through with financial discipline, and calls to share that they just closed on their first home. For the parent who faced her self-doubt, grew in her confidence, and followed her dream by creating a successful photography business. For each and every one of the parents who have worked hard to build a better life and future for their family.

The three years that I taught preschool at Sacajawea flew by. Then life took another unexpected turn. My principal came down to my classroom one afternoon and asked me to apply for an in-building kindergarten position that would be added the following year. I still remember exactly where I was standing when he asked me. As I was a full-time teacher who had been with the district for 26 years, it was almost guaranteed that the position would be mine if I applied. I wouldn't even have to pack up and move classrooms. The preschool program was moving at the end of the school year to a newly remodeled building. The new Early Learning Center would house all of the district preschools, and my current preschool room would become the new kindergarten classroom. I couldn't believe it. My dream had returned to me, I could once again be Linda Johnson, Sacajawea Elementary kindergarten teacher. I envisioned myself retiring in this room as a kindergarten teacher, just as

Inspirational stories from Washington's classrooms, featuring the Teachers, Principals, and Classified School Employees of the Year

21

I had always planned. I said yes, put in my application, and a week later the position was mine. My identity was restored. I rode the wave of congratulations from my colleagues and knew I should be happy.

But something wasn't right. I felt an unexpected sadness in my soul. It started small, barely perceptible. It grew as I met with my preschool families, and we created long-term plans to support their children and their families. I wondered who would take care of them next year. Would they love them as much as I did? At the end of the week, I received a heartfelt note from a parent. "Without you, I have no idea where we'd be right now. Thank you for the difference you make in our life." Innocently written, but perfectly timed.

At the end of the day, I said goodbye to my students for the weekend, looked around my classroom, and knew what I was meant to do. I took a deep breath and began to walk down the long, empty hallway. Identifying my emotions seemed next to impossible, my mind spinning with everything I needed to say. I entered my principal's office, shut the door firmly, and collapsed into the chair next to his desk.

"I'm leaving," I stated simply. Two words - changing the course of my teaching career, my world ending and beginning at the same time. Then the dam burst, and I dissolved into tears. Tears of relief and joy. I realized that my identity was no longer Linda Johnson, Sacajawea kindergarten teacher. It was Linda Johnson—educator and advocate for early childhood and family education. Four years later I will still tell you this is absolutely the hardest position I've ever had in my entire life. It is also, without a doubt, the most rewarding. I've found my passion and will spend my career capturing these glimmers of hope and celebrations of joy in my heart, knowing that we are making a difference, one family at a time.

Inspirational stories from Washington's classrooms, featuring the Teachers, Principals, and Classified School Employees of the Year

23

CINDY CROMWELL-SHOLTYS

2021 National Digital Principal of the Year

Kelso Virtual Academy
Kelso School District

Lessons From My Children

How my children have made me a better principal

I have had the privilege of working with some of the best educators you have never met. I have been surrounded by amazing, innovative, and driven role models my entire life who continue to shape me into the principal I am today. When I think of those educators who have guided and inspired me most throughout my 22 years as a principal, it was the outside-of-the-box thinking non-traditional educators. You know the educators I am talking about; they are the ones who constantly ask, "Why can't we?" or "What if we tried this?" They are the ones with a laser focus on demolishing barriers holding back students and those who work tirelessly to move obstacles out of the way.

However, some of my most impactful lessons come from my two teenage children Kenzi and Cooper. Watching them has taught me some lessons I reflect upon daily. Lessons to guide my way as a principal and person. As a parent I work hard to instill values, work ethic, and a passion for life within my children.

Inspirational stories from Washington's classrooms, featuring the Teachers, Principals, and Classified School Employees of the Year

25

Despite their youth, Kenzi and Cooper continue to be some of my most influential teachers and a source of inspiration.

Stand up and protect the important things. As a middle school student, Kenzi was home alone and witnessed someone rummaging through our truck in the driveway. Without hesitation or fear she ran outside and began yelling "Get out of here!" The thief dropped everything and ran off. Kenzi called 911 and provided the responding officer a full description and the direction the suspect ran. With her information law enforcement located the thief, made the arrest, and returned several stolen items back to their owners. We have had many discussions about the danger she put herself in, but her example of not hesitating to protect is powerful.

The lesson: Protect staff, students, and our profession without hesitation. Don't be afraid to stand up for those that don't have a voice or are without an opportunity to do so themselves.

Start slow, and then just do it. When my kids were learning to drive snowmobiles, they started out cautiously. Early on they learned how quickly the accelerator engaged, how wide turns had to be made, and the terrain of the area. After a bit of "safe" exploration they pushed the machine, let it run, and that's when they were able to experience the joy of the machine and the new landscape.

The lesson: It is important to get to know your situation before you engage and let the engines run to do what they and YOU were made for. But, don't wait too long or you might miss out on the adventure or the calling.

Laugh loud and laugh often. Kenzi has "that" laugh which can be heard amongst a cafeteria full of students. It's the loud "HA,

HA, HAAAA" that identifies she is present. In a crowded room you will hear the laugh before you see her. Some of her friends and brother at times give her the "shhhh" signal but that makes her laugh more.

The lesson: Laugh often, laugh loud, have fun, be known for joy, and don't let anyone tell you to stop.

Always be true to you. For "favorite decade day" at middle school Kenzi was the only student dressed up wearing a colonial day era costume. She was in a long dress, apron, and hat looking every bit like Abigail Adams. Her peers all chose the 70's, 80's and 90's with big hair, tie dye, bell bottoms, or MC Hammer style pants and looking more like Madonna or Cyndi Lauper. At Cooper's freshman homecoming dance he, like most of the other young men, wore suits and ties. However, unlike most of his peers he donned his favorite Red Sox cap the entire night and wore it proudly in every picture! Even after a few comments from those around him questioning the fashion statement he simply smiled and adjusted the hat.

The lesson: You can never fake who you are, and don't even try to pretend to be someone or something you are not. No matter the situation or event be real and who you were made to be.

Don't stop believing in the impossible. Kenzi was born a super preemie at 26 weeks one day into the pregnancy and given a 1% chance of being a "normal and healthy" child. Weighing 1 pound 14 ounces at birth, we repeatedly heard the statistics and odds against survivability. My husband and I understood the odds were against our tiny child, but hope guided us throughout her two months in the Neonatal Intensive Care Unit. On those rough days when she regressed in breathing and eating, we

Inspirational stories from Washington's classrooms, featuring the Teachers, Principals, and Classified School Employees of the Year

27

never gave up on her. We met with the medical team daily as milestones were monitored and next steps were planned. We knew the odds were slim, but we never gave up on our daughter or her medical team. At the age of three Kenzi received a clean bill of health at her last pediatric team appointment, and at age 17 she is as normal as a teenager can be.

The lesson: Research and science are important to acknowledge but don't EVER give up or assume the future for yourself, family, or students based on odds or likelihood. The impossible and unlikely can happen. Don't ever stop believing.

My children have provided me some of the most important lessons guiding my life's work within the principalship. No matter our situation or career path, we should never underestimate the unconventional wisdom of the out-of-the-box thinkers and those you are surrounded by every day. Often times those we are responsible for and instructing end up teaching us some of the most valuable lessons in our life.

SHREYA MEHTA

Student

Hanford High School
Richland School District

A Homecoming Court for Everyone

Student leaders collaborate to create a more inclusive tradition

A swastika drawn on a Pride flag, a man calling a transgender student a "thing" at a recent school board meeting, adults calling the LGBTQ+ community "he-she's" are all things that have happened during my tenure as ASB president along with the unfortunate usual lack of representation, f-slurs, and ignorance. So as Homecoming came along, I saw a golden opportunity to show queer students that they did have a place at Hanford. Over the course of a month, I spent hours developing a comprehensive plan to shift our royalty system from cis-heteronormative to gender-neutral to make more space for trans and gender-nonconforming students.

My proposal was generally accepted by the class until one student said, "If I won and was called Homecoming Royalty instead of Homecoming Princess I would feel like my identity

Inspirational stories from Washington's classrooms, featuring the Teachers, Principals, and Classified School Employees of the Year

29

as a woman was stripped." The floodgates then flew open and increasingly insensitive comments ensued as our leadership class turned into a battleground. Phrases like "there are no nonbinary people at Hanford," "even if I knew a gay person I wouldn't vote for them," and "what even ARE pronouns?" dominated the class discussion. Their words mirrored the larger conversations going on in our country about gender inclusive language, bathrooms, sports, and general fearmongering misdirected at the LGBTQ+ community.

It was a classroom culture war. My teacher entirely lost control of the class as we all fired shots at one another. In just one day, we'd all gone from friends planning the best COVID homecoming Washington had ever seen to hating each other.

I confronted my leadership teacher about his initial mismanagement of the situation, and he admitted that he was still completely new to the vocabularies I was using like "LGBTQ+," "pronouns," or "nonbinary," but he really wanted to learn and support all our students. The problem was bigger than in our leadership class, or at our school, it was in the lack of baseline knowledge about the LGBTQ+ community that stemmed from longstanding invisibility.

My conversation with him made me realize that every single argument being made was rooted in misunderstanding. In fact, the students opposed to gender-neutral royalty didn't really understand what it meant to hold a nonbinary identity. This knowledge gap was the biggest reason we were on different pages—changing the system felt like it was a threat rather than simply being more inclusive for students whose identities didn't fit inside "king" and "queen" labels. We had lost sight of one another in our misdirected anger. I changed my mindset and put an educator hat on.

I went to our school's student equity club, and I collected seven pages of firsthand accounts from LGBTQ+ students about the royalty system and general transphobia/homophobia at our school, alongside various news articles and blog posts from college and high schools across the country who had already switched to a gender-neutral royalty system.

The following day I went into leadership class not only with my research document, but also with a slideshow that highlighted everyone's common ground like "we all want to make homecoming special" and "we all want everyone to feel included." I carefully explained terminology and emphasized the importance of remembering that there are LGBTQ+ students in our school, student government, and certainly even within our leadership class.

Finally, we as a class made progress—together! While it was frustrating and invalidating at times, I knew I had a responsibility as a cis woman to advocate for my trans, nonbinary, and gender-nonconforming peers. Our class took a vote, and we agreed to try gender-neutral homecoming royalty.

It was a small difference, but a difference nonetheless. The students I worked with to bring about this change rejoiced. We'd used our student government power to make a systematic change. While this change was a little uncomfortable for many, by meeting people where they were we were able to start a new tradition of inclusion. At a future Eastern Washington leadership conference, ASB presidents in the area commended our school's efforts and noted that they wanted to take what we'd

Inspirational stories from Washington's classrooms, featuring the Teachers, Principals, and Classified School Employees of the Year

31

done back to their homecoming and prom celebrations. Even better, our leadership class had come together and listened to one another despite our initial differences. We'd looked beyond the trendy politics of today and actually met each other heart to heart. The praise from my fellow ASB presidents was nice, but it was more gratifying seeing nonbinary students get nominated without needing to force themself into a gender binary box for the first time in my school's history.

Homecoming night was beautiful. Audrey, a queer student who had won, looked stunning. Under her crown was cropped curly black hair, and she wore a sparkly black jumpsuit. What made my heart swell was seeing the huge pride flag around her neck. As she rode across the stadium in the back of a luxury car with the other homecoming royalty, the flag flew behind her like a cape, its colors only made more vibrant by the stadium lights. Her smile was contagious, and the crowd cheered madly. I knew the work had been worth it.

TAMMY LANPHERE OOMMEN

2021 Northwest ESD Regional Classified School Employee of the Year

Laventure Middle School
Mount Vernon School District

Unorthodox

An educator's advocacy for cultural competence is rooted in her experience as a mother

When your child comes home from school in tears and tells you that he doesn't want to go back, your heart breaks. When your son is called a racial name on the playground, or your daughter is called dirty by another girl, because her skin is brown, your heart just doesn't break, it shatters. You know that the only way for your children to get ahead is if you make sure they have the opportunities they need to succeed.

I knew marrying outside my community would have challenges, but to see and experience the inequities firsthand is something totally different. As a mother and educator of children of color, I learned from being in the trenches how important it is to give every opportunity for success to all our children. We need to change systems and beliefs that hold others back.

Inspirational stories from Washington's classrooms, featuring the Teachers, Principals, and Classified School Employees of the Year

33

My son came home from school one day in tears of frustration. The elementary school he attended changed the reading curriculum. He was now placed in a 2nd grade reading group while in the 4th grade. He had a lot of strong emotions. My husband and I were at a loss because every time we went to conferences, the teachers would say "Don't worry. He is fine, and he is such a nice boy." We would walk away irritated because we knew he was struggling with reading and writing.

Eventually, I sat him down and said, "Look, this is the deal." I took a deep breath and hoped what I was about to say would not backfire. "Look son, you should just drop out of school now." I paused and looked at his stunned and confused face.

He took his hands and cupped my face in them and said, ''Mom, I don't think parents are supposed to say that."

"Well, I will help you learn how to read, if you let me, because I know that the only way this is going to work is if you trust me on this."

He gave me a confused look; the one that says, "First, you tell me to drop out, and then you tell me to trust you?"

He said, "OK."

"Great, OK!" I responded.

I was eager to get started. I went to the school and asked his teachers what I could use to help him, but they turned out not to be helpful. I felt brushed off. At that time, educators were not looking at why students of color were failing. Instead, their parents were often viewed as not caring that their children were struggling and getting in trouble in class. This belief was based on false assumptions. Educators often held implicit biases that impacted students and their families. Many parents did not feel they could question their children's teachers. I was taught that teachers were the experts. I wish that I would have understood microaggressions and implicit biases. I couldn't name what I was seeing or experiencing at the time.

Well, I didn't give up. I went to the learning store and picked up phonics books and worksheets and read all I could. I was a paraeducator, so I knew that reading is a key to success. I had taught my sister how to read while I myself was learning to read as a child. It shocked my parents. They did not realize I had taught my little sister to read. This was not my first rodeo.

We started reading every night, and it was painful to get through the first page. He would read a line, and I would read a line. Then, he would read a paragraph, and I would read a paragraph. Pretty soon we were reading a whole chapter of The Island of the Blue Dolphins by Scott O'Dell. Every evening after school, I would have him write a paragraph of five sentences. We were consistent, and by the end of the year, he was reading at a 5th grade reading level. I soon found out that he had been placed in a reading group for English language learners. Someone had determined that because my husband was from another country, we didn't speak English in the home. I immediately had that changed too. My husband speaks four languages, and English is his dominant language.

Despite my son's misplacement, lack of support in school, and the large class sizes, his scores started improving and he was seeing progress. My unorthodox way of addressing the issue was paying off. I saw his confidence start to build. He continued to bring his dad and me his papers until finally he

Inspirational stories from Washington's classrooms, featuring the Teachers, Principals, and Classified School Employees of the Year

35

became a writer beyond my experience. He went on to achieve a Bachelor of Arts in economics and philosophy and a Master of Public Administration.

As a mother who has experienced her children's pain and struggles. I continue to fight for equity for families and their students who are struggling in school. Some children are academically misplaced because of assumptions about people of color and barriers that intentionally and historically were put in place to hold others back. My son was fortunate, because I was an educator, I had learned to access information. I knew how to navigate the broken system and had the means to do it. Many families do not. As a mother, I have started a Mothers of POC and Allies Support Group on Facebook. It is my hope to help mothers understand how to support their children of color in schools.

As an educational institution, we need to have accessible resources available to parents. We need to look at education in a holistic and humanistic way that meets people where they are and is open to looking inward at what privileges exist. We need legislators to understand and fully fund policies and programs that support the cultural wealth of our student population. We need to continue supporting employees' education opportunities around equity, diversity awareness, and biases This work is essential for our educators' competencies, the success of our students, and the health of our schools and society.

MARY KRZYSIAK

2022 Olympic ESD Regional Teacher of the Year

Dry Creek Elementary School
Port Angeles School District

Drop, Cover, and Hold
Finding hope in unsteady times

Today was the Great Washington Shakeout, a drill where students and educators across the state practice how to drop, cover, and hold in the event of an earthquake. We drop under a table for protection, cover our heads for extra support, and hold on to the table leg so the cover stays put. A three-minute drill officially prepared us for disaster: Simply drop, cover, and hold. Little did I know, I would experience a great shakeout with my students that very day in Room 4.

Ninety minutes after the drill, one of my students was sobbing after recess because she was slapped in the face by a classmate. We got out of the rain and back our classroom to sort it out as a class. As she shared her feelings, the student who hit her offered his apology. Hands began to raise as students shared experiences in their lives at home and school where someone hit them out of anger or retaliation.

Drop.

Inspirational stories from Washington's classrooms, featuring the Teachers, Principals, and Classified School Employees of the Year

37

This moment of vulnerable seven-year-olds talking through these difficult experiences and waiting to share their truth was as real as it gets. After someone shared that another student had used racist and derogatory language about his beloved auntie in front of his sister, he began to cry. Silence, and then a quiet voice rose from across the circle, "I'm sorry that happened to you, Jason."

Cover.

This moment stood still. You could feel the tension of the room release while the force of their shared stories offering comfort like a weighted blanket. My heart was filled and breaking simultaneously. There is no shakeout drill for this. Where was the table leg for us to hold on to for the cover to keep them safe? Amazingly, this class found it. This group of 20 seven-year-olds found their table leg through their shared stories of emotional and physical trauma. They echoed the sorries and shared ideas for how they feel better when things are scary. I sat with them on the carpet in awe. When they felt the rumbles and the ground shake beneath them, they found support through vulnerability and kindness. They found enormity in their smallness.

Hold.

We are teaching and learning in a pandemic. The public wants to believe we are back to normal because we are in school again but nothing is normal nor will it be again. Our communities have been shaken to the core since March 2020. Our young people are shouldering the weight of the pandemic, and we see the effects of this burden daily. But today I saw something else: Resilience. We are building it every day for our students by honoring their voices. Out of moments like this—born from trauma and fear, frustration and uncertainty—came strength. Empathy. Courage.

I often worry if our young people will know what to do if someone is not there to tell them to drop, cover, and hold when their world gets shaken upside down. But today reminded me that they will be okay. That we will all be okay. This generation is learning how to find strength and trust in each other, a skill we all need more of right now. On the day of the Great Shakeout, my students found connection through empathy, unity through support. And while there are many scary and mean things in the world today, there are countless examples of goodness and hope. And we could all use a little more of the hope I get to see every day from my students in Room 4.

Inspirational stories from Washington's classrooms, featuring the Teachers, Principals, and Classified School Employees of the Year

39

**JERAD KOEPP
(WUKCHUMNI)**

*2022 Washington State
Teacher of the Year*

North Thurston Public Schools

A District-Sized Classroom
A day in the life of a Native educator

"Hello? Sorry to interrupt class, but the district umm... Indian...is here to see...," says a visibly confused, apologetic, and slightly embarrassed school office professional. As they look to me for assurance, I smile and respond, "they'll know who it is." Common questions arise out of the chit chat as I await the Native student or students I'm there to visit with that day. "What is your actual title," someone asks to which I reply, "Native Student Program specialist." Usually, this sparks curiosity and a flurry of questions.

"What exactly is it you do?" Over the years, I've honed a few pitches including, "I provide cultural and academic support to roughly 230 Native American students in all 24 of our schools." Other times, I'll say something cheeky like, "I'm our district's one stop shop for all things Native American." It's true, though. In my role, I provide cultural education, academic support, work on district and state policy, and act as our district's tribal liaison to name a few of my many duties.

Inspirational stories from Washington's classrooms, featuring the Teachers, Principals, and Classified School Employees of the Year

41

Most inquiries are politely curious, though they can be incredulous. All of which illuminate the perpetuated invisibility of Native people in education. As a Native educator in Washington, I am one of .7% of Native American educators in my state. As a Native educator in Title VI Indian Education, I am one of fewer than 100 statewide. As a professional, I have to explain my position with a depth not asked of other teachers. I still respond with a sigh every time a non-Native reacts with surprise when learning that I'm certificated, too. One may wonder how one gets into Native education. Native educators have a highly specialized set of skills and knowledge that are rarely available in university. For example, I had to pay my way to Native education conferences, seek out teaching placements in tribal schools, and find opportunities to learn with Native people in, from, and with their homelands. I had to create and advocate for my own specialization throughout my teaching program. Native education is a calling with deeply personal inspiration for those of us Natives that pursue it. Native educators are some of the most talented and committed teachers and most overlooked.

While the person helping me in the office may not be acquainted with me, the students are. My general reception improves as staff see students of all ages light up when they recognize why they were called out of class. Even if I'm meeting a student for the first time, the Native youth with stronger cultural ties quickly notice cues like my beaded lanyard and express a general sense of connection.

Together we find our way to a commons, conference room, library, or maybe even an unused classroom. As Native people, we begin identifying relationality through tribal affiliation, relatives, friends, teachers, and sometimes ceremony. Through hallway chats like these, we quickly build a relationship. Even though we're from different tribes, we share common cultural understandings and experiences. "I worked with your cousin yesterday, and she said to tell you, 'hi,'" or "I've been emailing your dad, and he's happy for us to work together today," are common examples of how we establish legitimacy, trust, and relationality quickly. In individualistic worlds like the United States, people can get stuck on titles, expertise, and authority. For us, we want to know your people and who you come from first. The individual identity carries much less weight and knowing these sorts of cultural introductions are important. It's not that we all know each other. Though, I've had plenty of experiences with people who seem to think we do. Rather, it's through protocols like honoring our elders and all our relations, ceremonies, and gifting that we know about each other.

"I've been speaking with your teacher lately and she told me I just had to meet with you," is one way I help staff with transference of trust. This is one of my most common interventions. There is a long history of why many Native people lack trust in public education ranging from intergenerational trauma to public school's cultural misunderstanding and ignorance. This conversation starter is only for teachers really putting in the effort and is never a "gimmie." I've had plenty of frank conversations with students about enduring lackluster teachers. Starters like these are also key to my work. Native educators are so rare, we can't be with all our students all the time. We need allies, and we need to develop self-advocacy in our students. I'm always trying to educate and empower our ally teachers to be able to support them. It can be lonely being a Native student unsure of who in your school would understand your needs. Yet, if I'm not

Inspirational stories from Washington's classrooms, featuring the Teachers, Principals, and Classified School Employees of the Year

43

there and they know they have a teacher they can turn to, that student's world gets a little smaller and a lot more supportive.

Not every Native student is aware of their cultural identity or has had a chance to engage with it. It's not uncommon to inform a student for the first time that they are Native. Once we've settled in our temporary space and begin to unpack my activity for the day, I might say something like, "I saw that you're from such and such tribe." If it's apparent a student is hearing this for the first time, or even the first time outside of the home, we do a little exploration on their tribe.

Before we begin our activity, we talk about our materials and the importance of being in a good way whenever we make something. I talk about any cultural teachings and history that might be part of the project and wrap up with letting the student know that the first time we make something, it needs to be a gift. As we work, we chat about school, life, family, or a specific topic I was requested to talk about. Sometimes, I have a time limit to stay but usually I'm there as long as needed. The student is usually beaming with happiness and pride as we walk back to class proudly wearing or carrying what they made. It's still emotional for me to see a Native student proudly present their identity in school for the first time.

Occasionally, I'll receive an email from a family member overwhelmed with joy at the surprise or from a teacher who inevitably tells me they didn't know their student was Native. Both underscore the value of a typical day's work. The impact on teachers can be substantial as they start to see and look for Native students for the first time. They may reach out to me to guest teach one of their classes or refer more students to me. I might get a message from a teacher saying something like,

"I saw so and so with a canoe journey hoodie today. Are they in your program?" Sometimes I'll hear from a teacher who, recognizing there are Native students, expresses regret for the settler narratives they've perpetuated in their instruction or the superficial ways they've taught or not taught about Native experiences. Culturally responsive and culturally relevant education is the point of entry, it's not the end goal. We need to develop and support more culturally sustaining and revitalizing education opportunities for all of our students.

It's easy to spot an ally when, after watching what may seem like me chatting and laughing with students week after week, they compliment me for the work I'm doing. They recognize the power of connection, community, and developing a sense of place in an institution not built with our interests in mind. They see the students go from not doing any work in group to getting A's or even graduating early. They see students who have had behavior issues or wouldn't come to school become leaders. They see the value of making sure we have a place, patience for letting students learn when they're ready, and the power of culture. These allies can rarely explain what they see but know the transformation that comes out of supporting it wholeheartedly. When Native students can be themselves and supported with their unique cultural needs, all their assets are unlocked.

My work of supporting Native students raises visibility and awareness in the hopes that our children won't have to continue the same struggle. Several years ago, I guest taught a 3rd grade class. Afterwards, as the students lined up for recess, a proud, bright-eyed girl came up to me and told me she was Native, who her people were, and she was a dancer. Clearly, one of the

Inspirational stories from Washington's classrooms, featuring the Teachers, Principals, and Classified School Employees of the Year

45

few, or maybe the first, times she said that in school. After that heartwarming exchange, the substitute teacher thanked me for my presentation and with a sense of shock, told me she didn't know Native people still existed. With a friendly parting look I said, "well, there's at least one."

BECKY ADDERSON

2022 Northeast Washington ESD Regional Teacher of the Year

Lincoln Middle School
Pullman Public Schools

P.S. Can I Have a Jolly Rancher?

A place to belong

Several years ago, I was working as a special education teacher in a resource room. One day in late spring, I was working through my lunch break when the younger sister of one of my students walked into my classroom. Her eyes were downcast and red, her face showing signs of recent tears. Her shoulders slumped, and she appeared to be dragging her feet. I asked her if she was looking for her sister. She nodded. I told her that she was probably outside at recess and would be in here afterward. When the little girl looked around and worriedly out the door, I asked her if she wanted to wait. She nodded. I called up her teacher and told him where she was and went back to my paperwork. When I looked around, the little girl had squeezed herself in between two bookcases and curled up. I waited a few beats before picking up some Jolly Ranchers and making my way over to her. I offered her a variety of colors. She chose one, and I did too. I simply sat next to her on the floor, both of us sucking on a Jolly Rancher. Eventually her sister came in for her

Inspirational stories from Washington's classrooms, featuring the Teachers, Principals, and Classified School Employees of the Year

47

session, the girls talked for a minute and walked out together. Before the little girl left, she looked back and gave me a tentative smile. I smiled back and told her she'd be welcome anytime.

I would not know until later how much those words affected her. For the remainder of the year, she would drop by after school every so often to say hello, grab a Jolly Rancher, and even bring me a cupcake from her birthday celebration. Her smile always made my day just a tad brighter. A year later, after her older sister had moved on to middle school, that little girl's teacher came to me and asked me if I could help. The girl never brought back any of her reading homework, and the teacher was struggling to motivate her. Apparently, the girl talked of me often, and he wondered if I could help. I told him that he was welcome to use me as the "carrot" to dangle. If she wanted, and could bring back her homework completed every Friday, I'd have lunch with her. For the next two years, this arrangement continued. Almost every week that girl completed her assignments. Lunch and Jolly Ranchers became a common time between us. At first it was about her reading, then it became her bigger, more important projects as she continued to learn, grow, and be more independent. On her last day of 5th grade, she gave me a letter talking about how much she loved and appreciated me. At the end, she signed her name and added, "P.S. Can I have a Jolly Rancher?"

The lessons this girl taught me through our interactions have stayed with me since. Students who struggle or have difficult home lives are always looking for that place to belong. To be explicit, "belonging" does not mean students striving to fit in. "Belonging" in the classroom means students feel comfortable, welcome, and part of the classroom community. It wasn't until the year after my girl went off to middle school that I realized just how much I loved and looked forward to our lunches. For the longest time, I could not figure out what she got out of our time together, but I was finally able to realize that our conversations, although sometimes mundane and routine, were secondary to what was happening in the space. It was more about giving and receiving community from one another. She was able to talk to me about things happening in her life, both big and small. I was able to gain insight into her life and invest in her as a human being and a contributing member of society. Most importantly, I was able to learn and grow as an educator with her as a leading reason and example. I wanted to do my best by her, and because of that strong desire, I pushed myself to become better. Through her I learned how essential it is that as educators that we acknowledge and understand that need to belong. It is our right to feel a sense of belonging ourselves and our responsibility to foster that belonging for our students as caregivers of the next generation. Our schools' ability to nurture that sense of belonging will continue to play a central role in a child's development and ensure that students feel they belong.

Those times with our students when we make the most impact are not about the curriculum or the engaging activities. They are about being present and allowing the students to express themselves and to live in the moment. It's those little moments that mean so much to me as a teacher. It's about going to games, cheering during the recess pick up ball, and having lunch with kiddos who are struggling. It's about pausing and seeing those positives where they exist, checking in on a student later in the day after they've had a difficult moment. It's about sitting with them in the hall and letting them deal with their emotions in their own way and own time. And it's about simply being that

Inspirational stories from Washington's classrooms, featuring the Teachers, Principals, and Classified School Employees of the Year

49

"go-to" person; someone to talk to or to trouble-shoot issues with. Trust comes from repetition and great experiences. It comes from 180 days or more of relationship building and support. These little moments seem so simple to adults, but to our students these are the moments that can change a life, where they are fully "seen" and loved. If anytime a student needs to sit with me and enjoy a Jolly Rancher, I will be there for them—there to ensure they belong, are cared for, and loved.

RANDI KRIEG

2022 ESD 105 Regional Teacher of the Year

Goldendale Middle School
Goldendale School District

Mama Krieg

How putting relationships before content builds confident adults and scholars

I remember the day Sarah entered my classroom in her 7th grade year. She appeared somewhat shy with her eyes hiding behind her bangs. Right away, she showed a great interest for the content inside my classroom and the leadership opportunities outside of the classroom that our agriculture program had to offer. She attended livestock judging, soil judging, corn maze, served at the soup kitchen, and so on. I really can't remember an event that she didn't attend. And, it got to the point where she was calling me Mama Krieg.

As a part of my class, all students have to complete a Supervised Agricultural Education (SAE) project related to their personal interests and agriculture. Sarah and her good friend decided to complete an Agricultural Research SAE project. In class, the girls had learned about content related to Genetically Modified Organisms (GMOs), and they were interested in what the public knew about GMOs. So, I assisted them in writing and conducting a survey to distribute to the public. We went to our local grocery

Inspirational stories from Washington's classrooms, featuring the Teachers, Principals, and Classified School Employees of the Year

51

stores and surveyed our community as well as electronically distributed the survey to gather data.

The girls put in a lot of time and effort into their project. They competed locally and moved onto the State and National Agriscience Fairs two years in a row. On the trip to the state event her 8th grade year, I noticed that something wasn't quite right with Sarah. However, in the madness of the competition, I wasn't able to speak with her before she competed.

After she competed, Sarah told me about a fight she had with her mom. Thinking that it was just a typical mother-daughter fight, I tried to explain to her that I was sure it would all be better after her mom and her spoke. But, Sarah shared she was just slightly younger than her brother who had already been kicked out before. She was worried her mom would do the same to her. I think it was at this moment that I knew Sarah needed me to be more than her teacher; she needed me to be her mentor and friend.

Over the next year, Sarah competed in public speaking at the State and National Agriscience Fair. She continued to serve as an officer in Future Farmers of America (FFA) and even ASB. But, things didn't get any better at home. Sarah would tell me of situations she had been in that I had only seen in the movies. During her freshman year, Sarah's mom had left her without warning or communication and she was asked to live with her father. But, Sarah refused to move in with her dad. I remember watching her stand up in court, look the judge in the eye, and tell him why she couldn't leave our town to live with her dad. She talked about how involved she had become, especially in FFA, and how her "true" family who cared about her was here in our town. I cried not only because she said how the FFA and I had helped make her into a stronger, successful person. But, I cried because she was able to self-advocate with such confidence and powerful speech.

The judge ruled in favor of Sarah, and she ended up staying in our town. She had a grandmother that lived 30 minutes away and was willing to make sure she could still attend our school. Sarah continued to be very active in FFA, and I coached her in the Employment Skills competition in which participants go through the process of applying and interviewing for a job. At the end of her senior year, Sarah qualified for state in Employment Skills. This girl—who when I first met her couldn't even look me in the eye due to her bangs—was now a state competitor in a contest where you had to look the judge in the eye the whole time and sell yourself.

As I reflect on my six years of teaching and advising Sarah, I know that it was not the content that I taught Sarah in my classroom that made the difference in her life. It was the fact that I was able to get to know her as a person, serve as her role model, and build her up as a leader. I chose to invest in Sarah, and she chose to trust me to invest in her. The educators that make a real impact are the ones that understand the importance of relationships. Sarah is proof that if we choose to be a mentor and a friend to our students, we will forever be their Mama Krieg.

Inspirational stories from Washington's classrooms, featuring the Teachers, Principals, and Classified School Employees of the Year

53

SARAH MANUS

2022 Northwest ESD Regional Teacher of the Year

Everett High School
Everett Public Schools

Every Year I Want to Quit My Job

Spoiler alert: The pandemic hasn't made it any easier

As I sit here, seven months pregnant, waiting for my sick 2-year-old to wake from his nap, my news app alerts me that the Omicron variant may be reaching its peak. Another app tells me that I should receive my COVID test results within 48 hours. So I wait. A podcast tells me that every teacher in America is unsafe, while a TikTok informs me that skinny jeans are definitely out. Oh, and congratulations! My pregnancy app just let me know that my baby is now the size of a squash. #adorable

Every year I want to quit my job, but this year is different.

I don't have to tell you that. We all know it. We all feel it. We're all living it. We know about the burnout and the grind culture. We feel the capitalistic pressure to work through the strain of education's constantly changing and growing demands; the

Inspirational stories from Washington's classrooms, featuring the Teachers, Principals, and Classified School Employees of the Year

55

strain of an inherently oppressive system; another strain of the virus. This isn't new. It's been written about, hashtagged about, podcasted about. We all know by now that teachers are not okay, right?

My friends constantly ask me why I don't quit my job. How can this be sustainable? They worry about me. My family worries about me. If I had time to see a therapist, my therapist would worry about me. But that kind of "self-care" feels like a laughable luxury for someone like me, a pregnant-teacher-toddler mom, working and parenting through the pandemic, merely trying to survive each day and bring a baby into this world, preferably a little more human than gourd.

I have no inspiring anecdote, no self-care tips, no light-at-the-end-of-the-tunnel story about a student who overcame obstacles. I don't know how to keep us all from quitting our jobs. And the saddest thing is that it's always been this way. Our education system was designed to reward the few and add weight to the backs of those already burdened. The pandemic is simply providing a microscope to that burden. And we're on year three of this? How many times do we have to learn the same lesson?

If I were teaching this lesson in my classroom, re-teaching, again and again, seeing that my students still weren't getting it, what would I do? Would I shift my approach? Differentiate instruction? Provide more scaffolding? Backwards plan? Collaborate with my Professional Learning Community? Attend more professional development? Look to my administration?

At what point would I question the system? The environment? My own practice? My own motivation? At what point would I give up?

What would you do? How do we get the world to learn the lesson before we all quit our jobs?

An app tells me that my son is waking up from his nap.

I'm so relieved he isn't screaming, that his fever has gone down, that he's had a couple wet diapers today. That I had energy to load the dishwasher. That when I feel the baby inside me flutter, stretch, and kick, I'm forced to pause. Sometimes to sit. To breathe through the pain before I start the next thing.

This isn't some "what doesn't kill you makes you stronger" trope. But being pregnant does instigate reflection. And for me, as a mom, I've learned that I have to live in hope. It isn't a cute hashtag or some sub-genre on teacher TikTok. Hope is necessary for my survival. I can't make new life, embrace new life, sustain new life without some pretty fierce hope. I'm a learner. I lose curiosity without it. I'm a teacher. I facilitate learning because of it.

Why haven't I quit my job? What an impossible question to answer. I guess I'm good at it? I like kids…sometimes? When I feel the rush of collective learning, it's really good and really fun. But do those moments outweigh the burden of pandemic teaching? Logically and mathematically, no. Absolutely not. We need tangible, systemic changes to ease those burdens, and I will continue fighting for those changes for as long as I stay in this profession.

Inspirational stories from Washington's classrooms, featuring the Teachers, Principals, and Classified School Employees of the Year

57

But before I see those changes, I have to do me, or I can't do this job. And the only way I know how to do that is to practice hope. Daily, frustrating, painstaking hope. Not empty positivity, not blind optimism, but a very conscious, deliberate choice to believe that change is possible. That's my grind. That's my grit. If I don't have hope, I'm defeated before I even start. We have to be conscious of the possibility for change in order to pursue it. So for me, hope is step one. Everything else hinges upon it.

Hope starts as a form of planning. Then, it becomes a practice. I seek it out within my students: I look for the ways they continue to show up, so I continue to show up. I practice marveling at their curiosity, their persistence, their Gen Z quirks that both confound and hearten me. I practice noticing what impassions them, and it becomes what impassions me: the drive for more equitable opportunities, the pursuit of autonomy, the demand for a future that is more just than the present. Have you ever met anyone more enraged than a teenager? Through the lens of hope, that rage is passion. Their passion fuels my hope.

Over time, this hope becomes a mantra. A routine, a reminder, a ritual. The song you can't get out of your head, even when you're sick of it. To forget it would be to lose a small part of you, and you aren't going to let that happen, because at the end of the day, you know that tune is catchy as hell. Hope is that ineffable thing that keeps us grounded, keeps us going, maybe even makes us feel a little more human.

And I'm not sure there's an app for that.

SARNIKA ALI

Student

Auburn Riverside High School
Auburn School District

It Just Takes One Email

A student discovers their passion when they decide to reach outside of their community

I always had a knack for putting too many things on my plate, none of which I was particularly passionate or interested in. My free time was always given to numerous commitments in different clubs and activities at school, none which really made me particularly happy. I didn't have an interest in the National Honor Society club, key club, or math club. Frankly, they bored me. But if I wasn't pouring time into unnecessary clubs to fill up the extracurricular section of my college applications, I was watching Grey's Anatomy—again. I wanted my time to go somewhere useful, into something which can help me with my future endeavors. Essentially, I wanted my time to go into my passion, I just had no idea what it was. A dilemma I suppose most teenagers face and figure out at some point.

Although I was a flute player for five years, I wasn't really passionate about the music I was playing. The instrument just didn't feel like me, or at least that's what I told my family when I said I didn't want to continue playing flute. So I switched to bassoon, and my interest in music peaked instantly. Now music

Inspirational stories from Washington's classrooms, featuring the Teachers, Principals, and Classified School Employees of the Year

59

is a huge part of my daily life. Even my middle school band teacher said, "the bassoon really is the instrument for YOU." This led to my creation of a blog, my qualifications for different musical honors, and lots of loud bassoon practicing in the middle of the night which kept my family up.

I've always had an interest in mental health. Not just the general surface level where I see many of my peers chanting "It's okay to not be okay" and "mental health matters" as they continue to stigmatize and distance themselves from those struggling. I knew my interest and passion ran deeper than the toxic positivity I saw in those around me. My teacher also noticed this interest when I chose student mental health in high schools as the focus for my research in my junior year AP Seminar class. Granted, this research was just for a school project and an "A" in the gradebook to most of my peers, but for me this project really opened my eyes to the issues that caught my attention.

When my research was completed, I tried talking to my teacher about what I could do beyond the classroom with mental health advocacy and how I, as a 16-year-old, could make any sort of impact or difference in the communities that continue to stigmatize mental illness. And she said, "send an email." Now the apps I used on my phone never included my Gmail as they were primarily social media platforms. Gmail was more an app I had to turn on so I could see when my teachers posted a new assignment. So of course, I didn't understand what she meant at all. What could an email do? Yet, I still drafted one up on Google Docs and shared it with her so we could read it over and make edits. She then approved the email and said it was ready for sending.

From Seed to Apple

With my trembling hands, I clicked "send." Multiple times actually. I sent the same email to multiple people, hoping for a response from just one. An email about myself, my broader community, and the pressing issue regarding mental health in a vulnerable community of teenagers. To my surprise, I got responses from quite a few people who wanted to hear my opinion on youth mental health. A few weeks later, I was on a phone call with the chairman of the Washington State Board of Education. At that time, I had meetings being planned with my principal and counselors, the vice chair of the Board, a Program Supervisor at the Office of the Superintendent of Public Instruction. I had more emails out to professors at University of Washington and Forefront Suicide Prevention.

"Wow." That was the response I got from my teacher when I told her about my upcoming meetings. Now, instead of being nervous to email people I didn't know, I was nervous about prepping for the meetings that followed. Still, I didn't believe anything would change. After all, don't busy officials listen to people that they serve all the time and not act? However, a few of these meetings didn't just end at the listening stage. They ended with "I'll be in touch" or "Let me connect you with..." so I guessed somehow my work would continue.

Fast-forward to the end of 2021. In the 12 months since sending that email, I received an internship from a professor in equitable mental health care at one of the top schools on my college list and became a research assistant at another top-of-the-list university. I have been working on a research paper to submit for publication with professors at another college and got a full-time internship for the summer underneath a professor at my dream school. In addition to research opportunities, I also

Inspirational stories from Washington's classrooms, featuring the Teachers, Principals, and Classified School Employees of the Year

61

received a job at a company focusing on mental wellness and became the Co-Chair for a workgroup on the Washington State Suicide Prevention Plan for 2021.

The experiences I've been given are absolutely extraordinary. The best part is it's just the tip of the iceberg on the list of opportunities I've received. All in just the span of 12 months. I sent my first email on December 1, 2020. And let me say, on November 30th, 2020, the only thoughts in my head were if I should end the email with "Sincerely" or "Thank you for your time." By the way, I decided to stick with "Thank you for your time" because I thought it was less generic and more likely to get a response. If you asked me on the morning of December 1, I would've said, "yeah it's just an email" because I didn't think they were actually meaningful or important. I thought people only used their email when they grew up. I now wake up every morning, and the first thing I do is scan my notifications for emails. It's my most useful app and my favorite way to pass free time. I wake up excited to start my day because here I am, now seventeen, and making a profound impact in a field very significant to me.

I sent 13 emails on December 1. I only received seven responses. I got four meetings scheduled with six of the seven people who responded. And today, I can't handle the amount of emails I receive nor can I fit time into my schedule for new meetings. I never quite understood the saying "If you love what you do, you will never work a day in your life." I also didn't understand those who claimed that if you love what you do, it'd take hard work although you would persevere. Through the experiences and numerous emails I've sent, I've learned it's both. You love what you do, so you put in the work to succeed, yet it feels effortless because your passion is driving you to push forward.

So whether it is one email, one conversation, or one opportunity, take it. Whether you think it's important or not, whether you believe it'll make a difference or not, do it. Because at the end of the day, you might've done the one thing to find the spark within you that makes you excited to wake up in the morning, just as I found mine.

Inspirational stories from Washington's classrooms, featuring the Teachers, Principals, and Classified School Employees of the Year

63

About the Award Programs

Since 1963, the Washington State Teacher of the Year program has selected one outstanding educator annually to serve as the Washington State Teacher of the Year. The Teacher of the Year is selected from a slate of up to 9 regional candidates representing Washington's nine Educational Service Districts (ESDs) and including Tribal Schools. In 1963, 1970, 2007, 2013, and 2018, the state program garnered national attention when Elmon Ousley of Bellevue School District, Johnnie T. Dennis of Walla Walla School District, Andrea Peterson of Granite Falls School District, Jeff Charbonneau of Zillah School District, and Mandy Manning of Spokane School District, respectively, were each selected as the National Teacher of the Year.

Washington began naming Classified School Employees of the Year in 2010. In 2019, Congress passed the first national recognition program for classified school employees. The Recognizing Inspiring School Employees (RISE) award is run by the US Department of Education. In May 2021, the US Department of Education named Melito Ramirez of Walla Walla School District as the first ever National RISE Recipient. The Principal of the Year program is a project of the Association of Washington School Principals.

Anyone can nominate someone for Teacher, Classified School Employee, or Principal of the Year. Nominees complete a written application and enter the regional selection process. Each region recommends a regional finalist to the state program. The State Teacher, Classified School Employee, and Principal of the Year are selected from among these regional finalists by a committee made up of diverse educators, families, students, and education stakeholders.

Inspirational stories from Washington's classrooms, featuring the Teachers, Principals, and Classified School Employees of the Year

65